Garden
of
Thoughts

Garden of Thoughts

Poetry

NOAH WEAVER

A Red Raspberry Book

Red Raspberry Publishing LLC
5326 Lowell St
Mission, KS 66202

Red Raspberry takes great pride in the books and games they publish and are happily committed to helping make the world a more artistic place.

Book Cover designed by Arianna Neal and Noah Weaver
First edition published in 2023

Printed in USA

Dedicated to my mom and her
beautiful garden.

SALAD GARDEN

viii   Foreword

2   #1 Garden of Thoughts

3   I Begin to Write a Poem

6   #2 Wreckage

7   Mistakes

11   #3 In Relation to the Weather

12   The Calm of the Storm

14   Fall Leaves

15   The Birth of a Snowman

17   #4 Magic Numbers

18   Memories

23   The Fear of Failure

27   #5 Be Brave

28   Stress

31   #6 Relax

32   Moment in Time

35   The Teenage Years

39   X Marks the Spot

43   #7 Lighting the Way

44   Allegory

47   #8 Mountain Pass

48   Inner Demons Lie

52   #9 Friendly Neighbor

53   Response Poem to All Poets

58   Who's Gonna Stop Me?

62   #10 I Can Do This!

63   Every Step of the Way

66   #11 Counting Blessings

67   Diamonds are a Guy's Best Friend

FLOWER BED

72   #12 The Greatest Discovery

73   The Tree of Love

76   Are You Ready for Love?

81   Love is in the Air

86   Sitting in Your Heart

88   I Fall Fast

92   First Kisses

94   #13 Starlight in Her Smile

95   Lovely Sunday

96   Badass Brunette

98   A Thousand Burning Suns

101   #14 Together

ODDS & ENDS

104   #15 Nice to Meet You

105   I'M VEGAN

SUNSHINE & SHADE

114   Dreams

115   IMPOSSIBLE

116   The Saga Continues

117   A MIC

118   Right Writings

119   The Midnight Hour

120   Mankind

121   Punchlines

122   Waves

123   Brightside

124   The Quest

125   Love?

126   Ego

127   Do You?

128   Dizzy

129   Choices

130   I Love You

       Acknowledgements

Foreword

"Your friends don't hate you.
Your world is not collapsing.
Just drink some water."
- Haiku #6, "Relax," p. 31.

And guess what? He's right. So, before you get too far, fix a tall glass of water, and settle into your favorite chair. Grab a blanket. Whoever you are, wherever you are, today is going to be a good day. I say that confidently since you have made the decision to interact with this book. *Garden of Thoughts* is a collection of bright, inquisitive poetry that will almost inevitably brighten your mood and get you thinking more clearly. If you commit to patiently integrating the messages within these works, rest assured this book will strengthen you, empower you, heal you, nurture you.

My name is Gemma Campanini. I am a fellow poet, as well as a project/event facilitator within the writing community. I met Noah Weaver by accident. I do not remember the day. Our families were good friends before either of us were born, so our lifelong friendship slowly happened out of circumstance and frequent proximity. Needless to say, Noah and I have grown up together—not only as children, but also as artists. As adults, we continue to play a significant role in fostering each other's growth as writers and overall creative path-pavers. We did not always share that dynamic, however; I can recall the specific pivotal day when Noah and I became no longer simply friends, but full-blown creative comrades.

It was in April of 2015, when I began hosting a community project in Lake of the Ozarks, Missouri: an open mic night for original poetry called "Oh Snap Poetry," often shortened to just "Oh Snap." Since I was fifteen years old when I created this project, my family helped me with running this event (and they still do! Shout out to my awesome family). Also investing in the success of the new-at-the-time "Oh Snap" poetry night, Noah's family helped ours by driving three hours from Kansas City to attend the event and show support. After arriving at the coffee shop, Noah asked me where he could find the sign-up sheet. At that time, I was surprised. Noah writes poetry?

Hell *yes* he does. You should see what this guy can do (and soon, you will). Something profound happened to Noah on the "Oh Snap" stage. Before, he was someone who perhaps *had* written a few poems here and there… but from that day onward, Noah stepped into the shoes of a *lifelong* poet and wordsmith. The transformation was clear as day and happened before our very eyes. Something lit within him, a fire still burning through every page of *Garden of Thoughts.* I find his passion so beautiful, and I know you will too.

At the beginning of his life as a wordsmith and still to this day, what distinguishes Noah's poetry is the theme of resonant positivity he infuses through his work. Even when tackling difficult topics, as he occasionally does, his words display a commitment to uplifting others and offering warmth back into an otherwise cold topic or situation. Noah assists his readers or listeners in navigating the frustrations of adult life while rediscovering a youthful—but not naïve—sense of authenticity, trust, and play. Overall, Noah's poetry manifests itself as any combination of whimsical and lyrical, soft and sweet, deep and imploring–sometimes all of the above. Inside and outside of his writing, Noah gives the gift of instilling peace back into a chaotic world, abundance into a world of scarcity. These are the gifts he brings.

As you read this book, you will journey with Noah through not only the depths of his mind, but also through the pathways of your own. Because his work plunges so deeply into the human condition as a whole, certain pieces of his work are bound to propel you inadvertently into your own experiences. Be prepared for deep introspection and reflection as you journey forward with Noah.

In the work that follows, you will be led through reflections of personal attitude, relationships, humor, wit, tragedy, recovery, and deep emotional surrender. As you will soon see, Noah pours attention, care, and curiosity into every word. And in doing so, he pours his love directly into you. Noah's poems are there to inspire, to love, to create, and to be. Are you ready for a great journey? I think you are, and I thank you for taking this time. It is a decision you will not regret. By reading *Garden of Thoughts,* you are truly investing in your own wellbeing. So, take that drink of water we talked about earlier. Then buckle up, and let's take a drive through a beautiful *Garden of Thoughts.* While some prefer a speedy arrival, I say we take the scenic route.

Safe travels,
Gemma Campanini

SALAD GARDEN

Haiku #1
Garden of Thoughts

A garden of thoughts
can be peaceful or deadly.
What you grow matters.

I Begin to Write a Poem

I begin to write a poem.

Through my brain the metaphors fly thick'n'fast
Different combinations
Of everything I have learned in my past.

Typing, typing, typing,
Eh, it's not quite right. Select all, backspace.
Start over.

Through my brain the metaphors bounce, thick'n'quick,
Different combinations
Of everything I've learned in the last tick, tick, tick.

Typing, typing, typing, that's still not it.
Start over

The metaphors speed through thought so fast,
My fingers have to type like The Flash,
So I don't fall behind,
Or lose track of the words I find.
All things are forgotten with time.
Oh shoot!
What was that next line?
I just had it.

Salad Garden

Come on, come on.
It's on the tip of my tongue.
What was it?
What was it?

Dammit it's gone.

Writing a poem is so much harder than I thought.
I thought the thought process would come easy,
Ha!
I thought wrong, it does not.

Why did I think this would be a good idea?
A wordsmith I've never been.
Never forged with a pen.
Or foraged through the forest of words
And written my own down on trees.
I'm down on my knees,
Praying to Apollo, the greek god of poetry,
To please!
Inject my brain
With all the metaphors, cool phrases and sayings.

If I have to,
I will perform a seance to get him to speak to me.
Will that please The o'mighty god of poetry?

I want to move my heart onto a page,
So that others may gaze
At it's beauty and pain and all of the rage
That's trapped inside will be able to escape,

Run away into that forest of words
And carve itself onto paper thin trees.
So please!
Give me the abilities
To tap into my full potential
Apollo! Are you listening?

I long to pierce the page with my words
But they keep missing.

Hey, I liked that last line.
I think it's time to write a poem.
Maybe with a rhyme?

The metaphors fly, thick'n'quick
Through my mind,
twenty six characters as one combine
Into different combinations
Of everything I've learned in my life.

Haiku #2
Wreckage

It takes one shipwreck
to lose all of your treasure.
Years to find again.

Noah Weaver

Mistakes

You know, we all make mistakes.
We sweep them under the carpet,
Hide them behind the drapes.
Always pretending to be perfect.
But, if something's perfect it's usually fake.
Haven't we learned that, that doesn't work,
How much longer will it take?

Until we find that the more we hide,
The more we pretend to be mighty and high,
The more damage we do to ourselves
Our egos are, oh, so, sly.
Most mistakes are harmless,
But some are like birds falling from trees,
We break our wings.
Requiring healing before we can learn how to fly.

And, if we aren't careful, we'll never fly.
We'll just keep digging this hole,
Making mistakes by filling our soul,
With money and power,
Do we have a real goal?
Driving down this road alone
Because no one else will follow.

No matter how many loops we make
We pass that same troll,
We keep paying his toll,
The wheels go round and round,
Yet we never grow as we roll.
If we don't learn from our mistakes we'll be stuck in a lull.

History always repeats itself.
History always repeats itself.
History always repeats itself.
Until we break the cycle!

I've made so many mistakes,
And many of the mistakes I've made
Have kept me up at night.

Why did I say that?
Why did I do this?
Why can't I sleep?
Screw this.

Hey,
I made a mistake.
I messed up.
I am sorry.
I promise I'll try to learn and change
And if I don't you can bar me
From your life.

But, I'd hate to lose a friend,
They are what matter in the end,
Sticking with me through thick and thin,
When I'm frowning they make me grin!
Give me the strength to begin again,
My pride isn't worth losing a friend.
Or two,
Or three.

History always repeats itself.
History always repeats itself.
History always repeats itself.
Until I break this fucking trend!

I must learn from my past
So as my future moves past
I do not repeat the mistakes of my past
I'll keep failing until I've passed
On from my past
Enough knowledge that I may pass
The class known as my past
And permanently move past the past.
It's time to learn from and let die the mistakes of my past.
But, before I move on, I must ask,
Did you keep up? Or did I lose you, too, in the past?
Maybe, I should rewind and go back into the past,
Before this poem had begun let alone passed.

No!

I am done repeating the past.

It's high time I learn from the belly flops,
When my brain high dive drops,
So that someday I can finally stop

My history

Repeating itself.
Repeating itself.
Repeating itself.
Repeating itself.

I've learned my lesson.

Haiku #3
In Relation to the Weather

Welcome! Come in, Spring!
Your brother stayed a long time.
Winter is leaving.

The Calm of the Storm

The earth is swept in darkness.
Covered by a heavy, brooding blanket.
All is not peaceful under that cover.
The wind howls, the wolves run for shelter.
The owls hide their heads among their feathers,
buckling down for what they sense is coming.

Thunder cracks, and cracks of light break the sky,
Illuminating the world.
Revealing a young boy, age thirteen,
Smiling up to the heavens,
Daring them to show him what they can do.

His mother yells for him
"Come inside! You'll catch a cold once the rain hits"
He doesn't hear her,
Caught in the rapture of the storm.

He stoically stands his ground before the sky,
Staring into the massive gray abyss.
The excitement is building in his chest.
No way is he missing this!

He can feel the thunder in his veins;
The time grows near.
The sky shakes and quivers,
Still, he does not cower in fear.

Noah Weaver

He lives for the storm.
Standing in the rain
He feels at peace,
He feels at home.

Fall Leaves

I love this time of year,
Fall leaves start to hit the ground,
The wind picks them up
Whirls them all around.
It is a sight to behold and the sound.

Oh, the sound.
Takes your soul to a special place
Where all the bad thoughts get erased
You know how it feels when you can taste
The Autumn air as it briskly hits your face.

There's a nip to it that feels just right,
When it hits your skin in the dark of night.
It fills your heart and soul with delight,
Sends a shiver down your spine,
You feel no fright.

Leaves leave the tree
Thanks to a mighty gust of wind.
Pushed to break away
from the being they grew within.

This is that story's end.
A new adventure begins!
They are excited to be free,
But, they will miss their tree.

The Birth of a Snowman

I began this day as any other;
Laying on the ground no real form to speak of,
Just one humongous white mass covering all.

I hear voices,
Chirps of laughter,
And feel the tickle of tiny boots across my being.

Ever so slowly
I start to take form,
From flat to round
As if I myself were the earth
I am resting on.

These small creatures
With their high pitched, excited voices
Begin molding me to their own design.
Building me up, so that I may be.

One piece,
Then two,
Then three.

They put
Pebbles on my face
I forced a smile.

Added a carrot
My nose got cold.

Two pieces of coal
What a wonderful world
I saw before my eyes.

There I stood tall and proud.
Sticks for arms and round as can be,
I hope I get to *stick around.*

My smile; no longer forced.
What a world I was born into.

Haiku #4
Magic Numbers

Five, seven, five. What
five, seven, five can I make
with five, seven, five?

Memories

Hey, do you remember that time?
Yeah, don't you remember
How your mind captured the moment
Storing it away in your memory bank forever.
Don't you remember? Don't you remember?
I don't remember.

Were we scrolling through Facebook on our phones?
Maybe scrolling through Instagram on our phones?
Or maybe scrolling through twitter on our phones?
Oh!
We were playing that little game,
The one with all those bells and whistles
Designed to trigger our reward system.

Don't you remember?
Don't you remember?
You don't remember.
You don't remember experiencing any raw emotion
You didn't think to yourself
"One day I'll tell my kids and grandkids this story."
That will never create a story.

I could have been outside playing catch,
Catching up with friends,
Making new friends to laugh and share stories with.
I miss making memories out of moments.

I guess that will just have to wait 'til tomorrow.
Which somehow never shows up,
So this cycle repeats once more.

Lost in the world of the internet,
Losing the world of the intimate.
We've gotten to a point
Where our reality can be anything we want.
So, why do we choose to make it unimpactful?

Is it because we feel ease and certainty?
Knowing that nothing will happen in the virtual realm
That we can't handle with ease and certainty.
We run from what's happening currently,
Spend our time, our most valuable currency,
Hiding in the electrical currents.-We
Revolve around the next click
The next like, the next pic, quick
Fake smile for the camera! Click!
Which never makes us feel as good as we pray it will.

But, you know,
Something incredible happened today.
I looked at the sky and marveled that I
Could bear witness to something so real.
Thankful that I'd been given the ability to see
All this beauty continuously happening around me.

And yet even with this glorious field of vision
It's not unusual for me to spend multiple hours a day
Staring at this screen like it holds something new to me.

Something I need.
Why?
Because it's easy?
Because I feel safe?
Because I think that maybe...
If I don't pay attention to this world it can't hurt me.

I've come to the conclusion
That even if I hide from the world it keeps happening
I don't stop existing,
I stop living.

Really living,
Like feeling my heart thump a million miles an hour.
A feeling of thoroughbred horses jumping
Straight out of my chest
And stamping the ground in defiance
Of the blinders I've forced them to wear for so long.

I've come to that conclusion 10, 20, 30, 100 times now.

Yet I still keep repeating this mind numbing,
Childish wonder crushing habit.
But, this is the last time I swear,
I mean I really mean it this time man, I'm done.
I hate to admit this...but
That my friend sounds exactly like what I've said
To myself in the mirror countless nights before this one.

So if you see me staring sightlessly at this damn screen,
Tell me, make a scene, scream something obscene.

Wake me up!
Snap me out of this foggy nightmare of a dream.

"Yo man, what are you doing?!
You know this awesome thing called life?
You're missing it.

So what if it's impossible to understand.
I don't get it either,
That's what makes it all so fascinating.

Look, I know you're scared.
I'm right there with you.
I'm right here with you,
Come on man, get up
This day is only going to happen once,
Let's make it wonderful!
A day to tell your grandkids about.
Once we are done with this day
You will have a story,
So come on, let's get to it, what do you say?

Let's both remember this night, together

Store it in our memory banks,
Bank it for a far off rainy day
When we'll look back on this night,
As a night we will cherish forever

It's one of a kind,
Who knows what wild tales will come from this one singular night

Put down your phone.

Take a deep breath.

I know it can make you anxious,
Not knowing what's going to happen.

But I guarantee,
I promise you,
It will lead to something.

Something,
Something new,
Something exciting,
Something worth remembering."

The Fear of Failure

Hello everyone!
Thank you so much for coming out.
Now I know why you're all here…
You're here to learn how to overcome
The fear of failure.
And have I get the solution for you.

Never try anything new!

You can't fail unless you try!

Then again...you'll never succeed either,
Never live high,
Never be aloft,
You'll be like a sloth,
Slow-ly, me-an-der-ing, through, life, un-til, you, die.

Overcoming the notion that failure means you have lost.
You are finished. You're done.
Is the first step to overcoming
Every new obstacle you come across,
Mistakes making with finesse until you've won.

The heartbeat in your chest,
That is the rhythm of a champion.
Fail a hundred times
And you still have the strength to keep fighting.

Even though some may say it's over and done,
You know that
Success may come at one hundred and one.
Chasing your dreams 101.
You're going to fall flat.
Get back up, continue to run.

The key to success is learning from your mistakes,
Your missteps,
Gaining on your dreams
Trying to reach them
Before you come to an end in this race with death.
Don't be left with regret
As the last thing you taste
On your tongue in your dying breath.

And it will be.

Unless you chase
The thing that makes your heart beat faster.
You control your fate, you are your own master.
You will fail. At times you will collapse
And feel like your life has been a complete disaster.
A catastrophe.

Lift your chin up,
Wipe off the dirt, look to the horizon.
You will see
A light at the end of the tunnel.

Keep your eyes on the prize
And continue to rise to the occasion.
Do not despise your fellow humans
For the success stories they are makin'.

Write your own in words so bold
That everyone knows that you ain't fakin'!
That you goin' ham in life man,
You straight bacon!
You risk takin'.
So close to your dreams
That you're almost skyscrapin'.

Instead of regret,
Bittersweet
Will be the last taste on your breath.

Because the show is over,
But what a life you lived.
You lived it right,
Right to the end

To the end,
Where you met death,
Looked him straight in the eye,
Shook his hand,

"Hello, my old friend."

You do not try to bend yourself in half
To escape his grasp.
You sit in heaven,
Gazing down upon all the people
Blazing a new path.

Tripping,
Falling,
Raising their chin again and again
Smiling over their shoulder
At the aftermath.

And, you can't help but smile back.
You know they will succeed,
Because, they remind you of you.

You laugh.

Haiku #5
Be Brave

Emotions are tough,
trust, you will figure it out.
It's so brave to try.

Stress

I'm stressed out man!

Here I am
Once again,
Trying to create
The life I desire.

I was bored to tears for years
All because I was holding on
To the classic fears.

Fear of Failure,
Fear of success,
Fear that my future
Won't show up how I've pictured it dressed.

What if when I do quit my job?
Then boom!
Everything in my life falls apart at that moment?

Well I did quit that job.
Things didn't fall apart!
Well, not at that exact moment.
Actually things went pretty good for a while,
Then a couple of costly car situations later and
I'm stressed out man!

It feels like everything could go wrong at any time.
I have no spare funds. I'm down to my last dime.
I won't die with so many half baked ideas still inside.
Someday I pray to weave them with wordplay and rhyme.

I could write the world's greatest poetry book.
I could write a one hit wonder with a really catchy hook.
Get famous on the internet for my wittiest verse.
I've got so much to do 'fore I'm riding in my hearse.

I don't know why I'm stressed out man!
If I compare my life now to where I have been
I've got so much going for me,
Look, I'm so free with the pen,
I write write write.
My heart commands as much.
I must to show my love, my soul.
She deserves to know
How I come to life
When our hearts and bodies touch.

On my good days I know I'm human
Yet, I still feel like a fool when I get all worried,
I want to scream until my head is light,
My eyes are blurry.
I feel my mind spiraling,
Unwinding, it really unnerves me.
It's the worry,
That my life's going nowhere,
And it's getting there in a hurry.

Every passing moment feels like an opportunity lost,
Another coin flipped, another bad call on the toss.
What if I don't succeed at this dream,
What if at the top of my lungs I scream.
And, not a single soul is listening?
What if my dream ends up dying on it's cross?

And I snap back to reality and work that nine to five job,
Ope there goes gravity, I fall just like that coin I lobbed

Dammit tails again.
They tell me to keep my head up,
How can I?
With how quickly the world seems to spin.

I'm stressed out man!
I pride myself as a positive guy,
Earlier today I was happy.
I'm stressed out man!
And, I don't understand, why?

Haiku #6
Relax

Your friends don't hate you.
Your world is not collapsing.
Just drink some water.

Moment in Time

Love tender,
Live long,
Be kind,
Stay strong.

Live in this moment in time.
The future hasn't happened yet,
And the past is far behind.

Everyday is a new day.
So let's forget the old, start up the new.
When you do remember, remember the good times,
They can outweigh the bad few.

This moment is a gift.
We came up with the perfect name for it.

The present.
The future and past are just in our minds.
Nightmares and dreams to make us hesitant.
Because we think the future is where happiness lies,
Where we will find our vanilla skies,
Everything is perfect in the future.

Big, shiny, and new.
It makes it hard to remember that this moment
Is the only thing that's true.

And it's tough to focus on the present
When we are stuck remembering the hurt in our past,
When, this moment.
Yo this moment is where it's at!

We could be chilling like ice cream,
Living like fruit flies,
We've only got 'til Tuesday.
live like every moment counts.

1...2...3...
4...5...6...
7...8...9...
10...

Those ten moments are now over.
Gone with the wind.
So, let's spend our future moments
Breathing in their awesomeness!
  (Take a deep breath with me)

And the oxygen.
Deep into our lungs,
Feeling like we are floating on air,
Light and fly as a feather.

Oh, and one more thing,
Fuck the word forever.
Because the future and I'm speaking the truth,
It's all a lie.

Anything can happen. Anyone can live.
Anyone can die.
Focus on right now,
And it will put a smile on your face.

Just look around
Because, Oh Snap,
You are in a pretty cool place.
The past can make you stronger.

But, only if you remember the love,
Stop letting the pain leave you Frozen,
Let It Go!
You're not who you used to be,

And you should know, you can change your thoughts
At any time. The only you, lives right now.
Every past moment is just a story in your mind;
Of times long ago.

When, maybe the sun didn't shine.
Maybe times were hard,
Maybe you were mad.
But, what if that's just a story, and,

1...2...3...
4...5...6...
7...8...

This moment is all you had.

The Teenage Years

Ahh, the teenage years,
Perhaps the finest years for writing poetry.
All that raw, unfiltered emotion,
You haven't locked it away from the world,
Yet.
Locked it away out of fear that you'll be misunderstood.
Plus,
By that age you may have a decent grasp on language.

You're still you!
Still growing into your shoes.
Maybe, you haven't even had your first heartbreak.
You don't feel the need to hide
The side of you,
The side of you that you know to be true.
Out of that fear,
That if you show your true self
Someone won't love you for *you*.

You are still a sunshine yellow
You haven't had your heart turned icy blue.

Maybe I spoke too late.
Maybe you're on the flip side of the coin.
The dark side.
The heartbroken, lonely side.
The side that's covered in dirt and grime.

Salad Garden

If that's the case
Then this is the perfect time.
To expose your true self to the world
Time to flip this thing around and lift your head up.

Look at the brighter side of you.
You still shine.
Polishing your mind with kindness
Until it's brand spanking new.
You really are a dime!

I'm just giving my two cents here.
But despite your heartache
You won't break.
Stay true to yourself.
Even in lost love,
There is no such thing
As a bad mistake.

It's a learning process
You've got this.

But you don't need some poet telling you that.
Deep down, you know you're smarter than you think.
And, not just a smidge smarter,
The kicker is that, you are far wiser.

Good thing too, because you
Are at a crucial juncture of life,
Where choices are hard
And relationships are a trillion times harder.

There's a right path to take,
You can feel it in your heart.

You start down the road to your left,
No sooner do you begin your journey
Then doubt takes the wheel
And spins you around.

Until you don't know
Right from backwards
Or sideways from upside down.
Somehow in all this confusion,

You intrinsically know,
To take a deep look inside yourself
The outside world
Is spinning a million miles an hour.

But deep inside you, you find calm.
I think it's called,
Inner peace.
It gives you a chance to think, to feel what's real.

The world stops for no one.
But, you are not "no one."
You are *you*.
Your world
Will stop for *you*.

And good thing too!
You are always at a crucial juncture in your life.
Choices are always hard
And relationships shouldn't be harder.

The right ones make the tough choices easier.
There is a right path for you.
Once again, you start your journey,
Taking that first scary step to the left.

Feel doubt grab the wheel once again
Start to make your world spin.
Shake yourself free of that storm,
Follow your instincts and continue.

See what life has left for you today.
There is no shame
In finding out what's left, was not right,
You will learn from your mistakes.

Remember, there are no bad mistakes,
Passing up the chance to make one
Is turning away an opportunity.

That's the secret that doubt
Doesn't want you knowing about.

Once you discover this key, doubt will be powerless.
You are in control here.
You'll take your time, the path is yours.
You can spin your world at whatever speed you want.

Noah Weaver

X Marks the Spot

Everyone's looking for an escape.
A way to save the world
And all its worries for another day.
An abyss we can just fall into whenever
The real world becomes too much for us to take.

To my great dismay,
I have started resembling a horse with blinds on.
I spend my day looking down at my phone,
Avoiding the world around me,
As it may elicit powerful emotion
If I ever turn the lights on.

Same as the blinds,
My phone serves the purpose
Of making me dull to my purpose
But it's always there for me.

Always at my fingertips,
Always at my service,
It's been ingrained in my brain,
It's so hard to unlearn this.

Salad Garden

I've taken a deep dive into technology,
And it's time I come up for some air.
I can hardly breathe
I can feel for now...

But, each time I touch my phone
I feel I'm becoming more machine.

Emotions feel foreign,
I'm forgetting how to speak that ancient tongue,
They feel overwhelming,
I feel less love and I fear what I've become.

Cold,
Uncaring at times.
It's a rarity to find that gleam
When you stare deep into my eyes.

I'm only 23 years young.
Right now, I shouldn't be able to feel more alive.

But, here I am,
Standing outside on a perfect night,
And the sheer awesomeness of it is lost on me.

I used to give a shit.
Granted I didn't use the word shit
When I used to give a shit.
But, I used to give a shit.
Now why has the beauty gone
From the world when I look out at it?

I need to find my wonder again,
And I have a few moves in mind.
I made a map to follow, at the end,
I'm sure my treasure I will find.

First I will take a right
Where I left my worries on the table.

Walk out the door past my past self doubt.

Follow the path until I come to a fork in the road,
I'll lay my phone on the ground
And spin it to point the way.
I'll conveniently forget to pick it up again.

Continue down that course,
Stopping when the heavens start to change hue,
Set up camp
In time to watch the sun vanish from view.

I'll start to appreciate the joys of everyday,
A kitten purring.
My friends, making me laugh until my jaw hurts.
That special girl who makes my heart skip a beat.
Every moment I can spend on a baseball field.
A FUCKING SUNSET.

I will wake up at dawn, inhale a fresh start,
Start to become balanced within myself
So that I may breathe out all of my fears
As I no longer need them to keep me on my toes.

I'll stop teetering on the edge of maybe and what if.

Start down the road again,
Follow the signs that point towards
"Become who I need to be for me."

Swim through the sea of my future,
Staying afloat
By leaving behind what's weighing me down.

Climb the cliff of life's challenges.
Carrying only what makes it easier;

A bottle of water.
My friends helping-hands.
A rope made of my dreams.
Stakes engraved with the steps I need to take
So I don't fall further than I've come.
Lastly, a shovel to dig up the treasure.

I will persevere until I reach the summit,
I see it, there.
X marks the spot.

Is this my journey's end?
Will I finally find what I've been searching for?

Maybe my journey was what truly mattered
Suddenly I see the truth.
At last I see my treasure, I see peace.
I realize I'm happy with what I've already got.

Haiku #7
Lighting the Way

When the darkness falls
the moon becomes our beacon.
Our heavenly guide.

Allegory

Slam poetry,
As an art form is historically
Less about rhyming
And more about telling a story.

Vividly capturing each detail,
Glamorous or gory.
Like a hi-def I-spy puzzle,
Searching for the answers in this poem, this allegory.

But, me, you see, I'm all about the rhyme,
I was inspired to write poetry
By rappers who combine
Two, three or four syllables at a time.

Making sure each

Rhyme would chime in time with the rhythm.
While opening your mind to the world they live in.

So here's my attempt at just that.
Capturing the details
With Wordsworth a thousand pictures.
All while rhyming like I am the Cat in the Hat.

I'm trying to understand my own morals.
Wallowing them around like mouth watering morsels,
Swallowing, even though now…I find them unpalatable,
Trying to deny the growing taste that I am in fact fallible.

I used to have it all figured out, 'Mr. Happy Go Lucky'
Never had the urge to scream and shout,
Never before been so clouded with doubt,
I knew what my life was all about.

And now, I see multiple paths.
And I don't know which route
I need to take to survive this thing,
To make it out.

And, not just survive as in I'm stayin' alive.
But thrive, have a little pep in every step of my stride
I guess that's why they say life is a roller coaster.
You've got to be at least this tough to ride.

And, why they say life is like a river,
Go with the flow,
Conserve your energy
So as not to be swallowed by the tide.

Make it through the lulls and lows as it ebbs and flows,
Breaks you down, your tough exterior starts to erode.
But, there's no secret way out, there's no cheat code.
Life doesn't have easy. This is hardcore mode.

But that makes victory taste all the sweeter,
When you make it on your own
Not playing follow the leader.

Here you stand on higher ground.
It's a celebration raise your fist skyward bound.
To your amusement, park at the top;
Ride that wave all the way down.
Your success made the ocean so salty,
You could never drown.

Life is a roller coaster,
And you're a tycoon.

You've climbed that mountain.
Weathered that storm.
Survived that typhoon.

Those rocks,
That ride,
That ebb and flow.

Brought you so close to your sky
You could stand on tip toe, and touch…
The moon.

Noah Weaver

Haiku #8
Mountain Pass

The bone chill seeps in
Between mountains bathed in snow.
Alone, watch your step.

Inner Demons Lie

"She's going to leave you for another."
He says it with a snicker.
I feel it in my chest,
My heart burns a little brighter, beats a little quicker.

"You're not enough for her."
"As a matter of fact *you're not enough,* period."
He's always trying to taunt me.
Why must he continue to haunt me?

"Oh, and you think you have what it takes to make it?
As an artist?"
Here he goes again, he loves to start this.

"No one wants to listen.
You've got nothing important to say."
He tries everything, everything in his power
To take my self-empowerment away.

"Trust me man, I only have your best intentions in mind,
Kick back, relax, you'll never make it as a writer.
I am doing this to save you the headache,
I am doing this to save you from heartache.

We both know that love will never last
In the end, it's always a mistake.
You'll see that I'm right once it has past.

I mean, are you crazy?
Are you blind?
Are you some kind of buffoon?
The end will come. It won't be on your terms
And it will come far too soon.

She'll tire of your jealousy
One day, you'll have your last dance
With your angel under the moon."

Hey, demon, are you done here?
Blah blah blah, is all I ever hear.
Why don't you come out of the shadows.
Hello, what's this, do I, do I sense a tinge fear?

Are you afraid? Ready to fight?
I've not been in a fight all my life.
Yet,

For my love of life.
For my love of art.
For my love.
I will fight the good fight
Every. Single. Night.
Even against the odds,
Even if you're the one holding the knife.

My pen will be my sword,
If that's what it takes.
I now know the stakes, if I listen to you, let you win.
My heart, my soul will surely break.

Then you'll put me back together,
Hide my spirit away as spoils, I will be your treasure.
You'll lock me inside your Pandora's Box.

No, not today, not any day.
Especially not after I slice, dice and knock you right
Out of those atrocious, fiery yellow socks.

Do you want my attention?
Are you the one that's jealous?
My artistry and my lover have my passion.
Being the one left out in the rain is never fun.

Oh, that's your secret, that's the key!
You're the one who's jealous of me, now I see.
We all want to be loved, even demons.
Well demon, I forgive you.

But, I have to move on, I choose my path,
And I choose the future that includes
Being an inspiring artist. The future that includes
My love holding me,
Speaking truth to me
"You are the one for me, Noah.
You are enough. In fact, you are far beyond
What the word 'enough' could ever mean."

I see her heart in her words,
There's no debate in her mind.
No quiver in her voice. I'm head over heels for her.
And, she too is head over heels in love with her choice.

My dear demon you will find the one
The one whose right and able to love you.
Able to love true
But, it's not me, I'm moving on with my
life

We took different paths.
You relish anger,
I relish love
I desire to have reason to laugh,
To sing with the doves.

The story of love continues on,
Through the darkest dusk
And the brightest dawn
Existing in the oldest tortoise
Beating strong in the youngest fawn.

You can't stop true love.

I don't want to hurt you,
I hope you find peace
Whatever you choose, please know that
This is a fight you can't win.

It's not to late to change.

Haiku #9
Friendly Neighbor

I was at death's door,
I knocked, then I changed my mind,
Turned and walked away.

Response Poem to All Poets

Damn.
I mean, damn.

I have never heard words spoken in such a way before.
Similes, analogies, metaphors.
Crafted by wondrous wordsmiths
Who learned from previous poet's words.

This trade is passed down through the generations,
Like the very words we write.
Passed down from mind, through body, to pen, to paper,
With the power of a hammer striking anvil.
Crafting a sword out of the pen held in hand.

A sword so powerful that when it strikes,
It does not kill. No, it brings dead thoughts back to life.

Clashing with our mighty minds
To create a spark! Of imagination,
And, bring to light the demons we all hold inside.

Oh the wondrous words I have heard.
Spun through the air
And woven together like tapestries from times of old.
Poets painting powerful pictures,
About the past, present, and what the future may hold.
Thoughts never before had, never before told.

Let that sink in for a little while...

No one has ever thought quite like you,
Poet.

I mean people have been close.
But, you are as unique as a snowflake,
And not even God can copy those perfectly.

I have seen so many mics turned to gold,
It's like
King Midas is in the building.

I'm just blown away.
Imagine the feeling of standing in the eye of a hurricane;
Perfectly safe,
Perfectly still.

It holds you, surrounds you, but does not hurt you,
While you feel the world whipping wildly around you.
Hard to picture right?

Well when words were wielded weaponry
To strike down bigotry and bring about change.
I experienced a hurricane of new ideas in my brain.
And you are never going to be quite the same
After an experience that insane.

So to every poet who on this fine night,
Showed us that nothing is finite.
By giving us new insight,
In hues of both dark and light.
When they allowed their words to take flight,
On to this mic.

You are what the world needs.

And, from the heart beating
With newfound purpose in my chest.
To the hair follicles all over my arms
That you made tingle and stand straight to attention,
When your words gave me no choice
But to give them my full undivided attention.

Thank you.

You have inspired the poet in me.
I was unable to open myself up to write,
Until I had first opened my ears up and heard;
The beauty that could come from 17 syllables.

Or perhaps an epic 6 minute poem by George Watsky
About being a high school virgin, that made me
Throw my V in the air for the first time!
And brought to life the poet inside me.

There is a poet in all of our hearts,
Madly type type typing away,
Anytime we feel anything.
Every time we feel
All of the words that we do not say.

They tend to hide in the shadows,
Until they hear another poet speak up
And show them how to find their own voice
In their own way.

And, when they do find it,
God dammit it is a sight to behold.

They find it
With

The beauty of a school of fish moving in unison.
The majesty of a pride of lions atop rocks.
The deafening roar of thousands of birds all singing
The madness in their bleeding hearts at the same
Moment in Time.

Every time you share with the world
The voice of your heart.
Soothing spirits across the globe.
Showing, we aren't so different.
We aren't so far apart.

Inspiring other minds to share
The inner workings of their world.

Fun fact;
Our world is seventy one percent water,
One hundred percent art.

Keep open ears and keep opening hearts.

Because
More so than

Kings.
Gods.
Authorities.

Poets,
We have the power to bring the world to its knees.

Who's Gonna Stop Me?

It's time I take a good long look in the mirror
And decide who I am going to be.
Am I going to cower in fear?
Let my life live me?

Or am I going to take these reins
And ride off into my own gorgeous sunset!

I have been so passive,
Not aggressive in my chase.
Just chilling,
While the things I truly desire
Are screaming in my face!

Taunting me, "I bet you can't catch us!
Everyday, you sit there on standby,
We are getting further away
And now we can barely be seen by the naked eye."

Well they finally provoked me,
I've got to try!
I won't have a life of just getting by.
I want to be able to look back
Then look at where I stand,
Smile up at the crowd in that stadium and say
"I made it. My, oh my."

It's a hard choice to make,
I've got to come to grips that for the moment,
Free time will be a thing of the past,
Until I become one of the greats.

My entire life is at stake,
A happy existence
Or a smile, a practiced smile,
Completely fake.

Well I won't have that heartache.
Today I'm changing my future.
That sunset looks glorious.
It's time I grab those reins,
I want to live more like this.

I've got this little motto,
I'm going to start living by,
But it does have a bit of backstory.
"Let me 'splain, no there is too much, let me sum up."

In my favorite book series, The Ranger's Apprentice,
Rangers are masters of the bow,
As well as unseen and silent movement.
All traits I wish to be proficient in
For no other reason than they are awesome!
Anyway, how do they do it,
How did they get so damn good?
Well the answer is simple.
Practice, practice, practice,
And more practice.

And then even more practice.
Their lives hang in the balance
Of performing perfectly under pressure.

In a less dangerous, yet still in a sense of the words,
"Life threatening way," so does mine.
I'm going to adopt their motto.
"An ordinary person practices until he gets it right,
A Ranger practices until he never gets it wrong."

That's the way to live!
Give *it*, everything you've got.
Don't let something insignificant,
Like you failing
Be the thing that makes you stop.
Give your body, mind and soul
To the passion of your heart.
No one's ever said, "It's an easy thing to start."

Excuse me my friends,
I'm going to go yell at my mirror.

Get the hell out of my way!
I'm on this path no matter what you say.

It will save you some energy
To know that you won't budge me.
My mind is made up.
I will not be moved!
On my path, I'll stay.

No longer succumbing to the taunting chant of fear,
Telling me mediocre is good enough
That I'd be best to not risk anything,
Not risk my good, average life and stay put, stay here.

Well, do you see that turn in the road?
One, five, maybe ten years ahead
I want to see what's around that bend.
And, judging from the distance.
There are a lot of steps I need to take.

Five hundred twenty five million, six hundred thousand.
To be exact.
But, that's the road for me.
My reflection is the past.
I see that now.

The future is unknown,
Risky,
A complete mystery.
Coincidentally,
That's how all great adventures begin.

I can't wait any longer!
It's time I take that first step.
So, I'll be seeing you,
I'll be seeing you around the bend.

Haiku #10
I Can Do This!

Believe in myself?
That's what I'm trying to do,
It's just so scary.

Every Step of the Way

It's time I tell you about the car wreck I experienced,
I flipped my car on the guardrail, I was going 75.
It's a miracle you're hearing this.
It's even impressive that I can say it.
I made it.

And where I am today,
I wouldn't be here
If not for every person who helped me
Literally every step of the way.

Yes, I had the drive,
I wanted to do it,
But to my mindset,
They were the glue to it.

They held it all together.
They raised me up every day.
So to them,
Thank you, is all I can ever say.
You're amazing.
It's because of you that I'm standing here today.

So thank you.
I look at each of you as a friend,
It makes me a little bit sad
That our time together is about to come to an end.

When I leave rehabilitation, you will never be forgotten.
After all it's because of you
My legs are able to straighten, and to bend.
You're the reason I can walk and talk as fluently again.

Thank you,
Rachel, for the ability to say these words.
Thank you,
Jessica, for the gift of my freedom.
Thank you,
Jacob and Karen,
For my legs and arms, and the return of their function,
I need them.

You've all been fantastic!!!

To the nurses, I mean curses!
You're the best!
I'm not going to list you all by name
Because you are too numerous to list and lest

I forgot one.
For that amazing soul that would be no fun.
You've *all* made me feel less alone,
So many, many miles from my home.

I feel I've found a second family.
You've made it much easier to deal with this calamity.

You've asked me "are you okay?"
And even if I wasn't at the moment,
You made me feel a little better.
You have been and continue to be that vital component.

I'm thankful to you all.
You were there when I needed help,
You answered the call.
And, eventually with you by my side
I was able to walk down the hall.
You know by my side to talk to.
But, also to make sure I didn't fall.

So to every single one of you, therapist or nurses alike,
I made this poem to say,
Thank you.

It's because of you I can take a hike.
Or finally accomplish my childhood dream
And learn to ride a bike,
In fact,
It's because of you
That I'm able to *stand* and *say* this poem,
here on this mic.

Haiku #11
Counting Blessings

After the car crash
Each step is a miracle,
I always count stairs.

Diamonds are a Guy's Best Friend

Diamonds are a guy's best friend.

I'm talking of course about Baseball diamonds.

Be it the Royals stadium or the Sandlot.
It is a field of dreams,
Where legends and memories are made.

The best diamonds are made with real grass.
And, my friend, this is one of those!
The type of field that you look at,
And you want to run and dive, have fun, be alive!

The entire diamond is a brilliant emerald green,
Minus the warning track and the base path.

Which, I might add
Is the sexiest path you will run in your entire life.

I mean you touch
First base,
Second base,
Third base,
You may even go all the way!
Scoring the game winning run at the plate.

Who knows what could happen?

And, the warning track.

That is where we remember the greats.
The place highlight reels are made.
Where legends remain day after day
In the mind of every dreamer who saw them make,
"Wow, what a play."

Heroes are remembered,
But legends never die.

You may end up on that highlight reel.

If you jump real high,
Reel the ball back into the ballpark
By barely catching it on the tip of your glove,
Resembling a cold, delicious, snow cone.

The victory of catching that ball will be just as sweet
As the previously described snow cone.

A legend made in the blink of an eye
As you track the ball
To your glove with an unblinking eye.
Making half the crowd roar!
And the other half sigh...

You will want more!

The next inning,
Diving into home off of a line drive hit to right field,
You barely beat out the throw
To score the second run of the inning,
Giving your team the lead.

You will want more!

When your pitcher comes in to close out the game,
And there are two outs,
Runners on first and second base,
The other team's clean up hitter struts up to the plate.
The bat held with ease over his left shoulder.

Come on, come on, give me more!

Strike one!
A swing and a miss on a high and tight pitch.
I guarantee he tried to hit it for a game-ending home run.

You are way out in center field,
And you are certain the pitcher,
And the entire stadium for that matter,
Can hear your heart pounding.

More!!

Strike two!
Your pitcher came back with a curve ball low and away,
Barely grazing the outside corner.
It caught the hitter off guard and he didn't even swing.
Your heart is beating
Faster and faster and faster and faster!

More. More! More!! More!!!

It's all on the line.
This next pitch could make or break the game.
Your pitcher starts his windup,
You drop into a crouch like a tiger stalking it's prey.
More than ready to make the play,
No matter how impossible it may seem
When the ball gets hit your way.

"Swing and a line drive,
Hard hit to center field!
The ball bounces off the wall.
Noah Weaver is there to pick it up
He turns and fires on a line!
One run scores, here comes Finch rounding 3rd
The throw to the plate will be...
In time!
He's out! This game is tied
And after nine we are heading into extra innings!"

Need I say more?

Flower Bed

Haiku #12
The Greatest Discovery

I discovered love
like cavemen discovered fire.
It burned, then it soothed.

Noah Weaver

The Tree of Love

Do you remember being a kid and trying to climb a tree?
A branch broke,
The moment you shifted all of your weight to it.
When that branch broke,
Your trust broke,
Your trust in that tree and trees as a whole.
As you fell.
You felt an array of emotions
Shock, despair, dismay.
You hit the ground, sprained your ankle,
Bruised your arm, scraped your knee.

That tree became larger than life,
It took a lot more gumption to climb.
You were always worried about branches breaking.
About scrapes, bruises, sprains and various pains,
About all that aching.
But, you'd put on a brave face and climb once more,
Climb high, higher than before.

You'd show the world,
And the important part,
You'd show yourself, you weren't afraid.
At least not scared enough to let the fear lead the way
You would face the thing
That sent your heart hammering.

Flower Bed

You recognized that you must,
You loved the view from up there
And the climb was always such a rush.

A branch snaps!
You gasp, you grasp the tree
Catching yourself just before you fall.
Did you catch the tree, or maybe she caught you?

Fear screws your eyes shut,
You cling to the tree for dear life.
Eventually, you manage to open your eyes,
Oh, this is so worth it.

Up here the view is beautiful,
The sky is such a brilliant blue.
More brilliant than you'd ever believed it could be.
Today's a new day!
The tree sends your heart hammering
In a new way.

From time to time,
You still look over your shoulder at your shadow, your fear.
Occasionally you check your grip,
To confirm the security of the tree.

Cautiously, you resume your climb,
You get more brazen with time,
'Til you're striding,
Practically gliding from limb to limb.

The path is not clear cut, it's not even always going up,
It goes sideways, it goes down, it twists around.
Whichever direction, you gain new perception.
Which upon reflection,
Gave you more confidence for the next step.

Sometimes your mind plays tricks on you.
Makes you believe the branch you're on
Is about to give way beneath your fingertips,
Your muscles tighten.

When bracing for impact this is the natural response.
The tree whispers to you,
"Relax little one, soften that furrowed brow,
You are safe.
I will not let you fall, not now."

You hear her crooning to you,
Her soft breeze soothing you.
You know her speech is true,
That doesn't make it easy to believe.
You have been bruised before.

Why do you still risk being up in the tree?
Why not return to the safety
Of the ground beneath your feet?
Why face your fear of heights?

The answer is easy,
The answer is so easy for you.
You are in love with the view.

Are You Ready for Love?

The only difference between living and loving,
Is the letter I and the letter O. And, the letter U
If you choose to spell it differently.
Maybe that's the best type of love.

The type that you spelled incorrectly, intentionally.
The type that life wants to spell check
But you won't let it,
Because, your luv is unique.
And, you don't need other people
To be able to read it for it to be real.

Love doesn't always make sense.
All you know
Is when you are together, she makes you feel so alive!
Makes you feel like the sun shines brighter.

Maybe, if you're more the singing in the rain type
The pitter patter on the roof of your mind
Calms down as she speaks.
And, the pitter patter of your heart when she's around…

It makes you weak at the knees, makes you feel.
Makes you believe that maybe there is a god out there.
Because, something pushed us together, you and me.
And, if I saw it, I don't know what I would see,
But I could never disagree with whatever it could be.

Because you, made Living, Loving again.
I
O
U
Everything.

Maybe things won't work out between you and I.
Maybe we'll get into one, two, many fights.
Maybe we'll find our souls don't really see eye to eye.
We don't know where we'll be in two years or three.
People keep evolving.
Nothing's ever really the same as it was a moment ago.

Every tree on the planet has grown,
Every heart has become more its own,
Every stone that gets thrown
Into the sea of love creates ripples.

Until they find another wave
From another rock, to rock the same boat,
Then calm each other down,
When their two bodies of water collide
On the other side of that riptide.

Love is not to be taken lightly.
So I have to ask.
Are you ready for love?
You might be.
Because every tear is worth it,
The fear and the struggle,
It's all worth it.

It may cause pain and trouble.
But, there is nothing in this world that compares
To falling asleep,
Running your fingers through their angel-like hair.
Looking into their eyes, shining in the moonlight,
Touching their head and saying,
"Darling, I love what's up there."

Are you ready for love?

Are you ready to have your heart ripped out
When she walks out your door?
Then put back in
When she comes back to kiss you once more?

Her kiss, better than any present,
A king could give to a peasant.
You're so thrilled she's here in the present.
Use this as a chance to breath in her essence,
A fragrance oh so pleasant.
To get your fix
Until the next time you're in her presence.

Are you ready to get rid of all doubt,
To hear her deepest most personal of thoughts,
That for so long you sought?

Do you think upon hearing those
You'll still be ready for true love
That with all your heart you fought?

News flash.
We can think we're ready for love all we want,
We're not.

Love is felt, not thought.
Love will overwhelm your mind
And go straight for your heart,
No matter how smart you are.
Love is not something that can be taught.

You have to experience it first hand,
And it will stretch you thin,
May break you in two, but if it is true
You will bounce back like a rubber band.

Love will cut deep into your heart,
True love has the healing power of a certain x-man.
So no matter how deep you get cut the night before

Every morning feels like a fresh start.
It's worth it.
As the saying goes,
It's better to have loved and lost
Than never to have loved at all.

Love will reach out a hand
When it thinks you stand a chance.
It sees you wearing a suit and tie
And your brand new pants.

Flower Bed

You take love's hand and stand
Because this may be your final dance,
In this overpopulated, over complicated
World of romance.

Love is in the Air

You know I still remember our first kiss,
My first *real* kiss.
Ahh, our first kiss,
Eight days after our first date.

I went over to your house
And we were on your bed,
Watching Doctor Who on your laptop.

After we watched a couple of episodes,
We sat in silence for a short time,
It felt like an eternity.
My brain was humming.

I was trying to think of the best way to kiss you.
I settled in the end,
On asking,
"Can I kiss you?"

A million thoughts flashed through my brain
And that's what I came up with.

Hey, sometimes simplicity is best.
You said "yes."
I regrettably,
Was not at the right angle
To go in for that very important kiss.

Instead of re-positioning myself
At such a key moment as this
I awkwardly craned my neck up to you
Attempting to lock my lips with yours.
After I 'succeeded' I thought to myself

*"Oh god that was definitely the worst first kiss ever.
I have to redeem myself."*

So, suavely I said
"Can I try that again?" Miraculously you said, "yes." Again.
I found the right angle
And found much greater success.

Those were the first and second of many
Intimate conversations our lips
And soon our tongues would share together.

Nothing else in the world mattered when I kissed you.

The first time I said, "I love you!"
We were on my trampoline,
Just a couple of kids.
I took the leap and said it first.

You said "I love you, too!"
My heart leapt in my chest
And screamed "*Yes!*"
We rolled around and kissed, saying
I love you I love you I love you I love you I love you.
More times than anyone could count.

Releasing the words
Like so many doves who were now free to fly.

Near the end of our time together,
All of those, "I love yous."
Flying off on their new wings
Eventually returned home
To be locked in my heart,
The key was thrown.

I searched but was unable to find it.
With time I know locks become broken, unyielding.

I didn't roll around with you on trampolines
Or kiss you passionately anymore.
We stopped being the air in each other's lungs
The spark between us was extinguished.

No matter how badly I wanted
To keep it alive
Our fire died out.
The empty space where it was, was heavy,
Too heavy for us to continue bearing it's weight.

Those doves in my heart,
Long to be freed,
To fly on new wings once more.
But alas, I have lost the key,
My heart cannot be opened.

Flower Bed

So they pound inside of me,
Hurting, screaming,
Begging to be free.
My broken heart
Is what it sounds like when doves cry.

Their cries cause me pain.
I don't want to hold them trapped and hurt inside me.
I want to release them to the world.
I pray for my heart to sing again!

I have this dream,
That one day I'll release the doves,
Like a tacky Las Vegas magic trick.
One problem,
No one in the audience has found the key.
And I can't do this trick alone.

Until someone does find my key
I will do my best to take care of my doves,
Hold them close, try to keep them warm
And tell them like small children
"Everything will be alright."

Tell them that they will get the chance to fly again.
But until that happens,
They need to find peace within my chest.
Allow my ribcage to transform into a sanctuary.

Let the rhythm of my heart bring them peace
Lull them into deep slumber.
Give them strength
So that when the time comes.

They can fly with everything they've got.
And, you know what, it will be magic.

Do not forget the past little doves.
Remember fondly those feelings of love.
Soft skin on my palms and fingertips.

Sparks dancing back and forth
Between tongues speaking in tongues
That only true love understands.

You feel pain right now.
That pain will subside soon enough,
And with time the broken lock to my chest,

Your cage, our heart will be fixed
And once that happens,
Someone, somewhere, will find the key,
Turn it,
And,
Love will once again fill the air.

Sitting in Your Heart

Sitting in your heart,
I have the most amazing view.
I can see the inner workings of your soul.
A little bit of your rib cage too.

Your body is a work of art.
And as if that weren't enough,
Your mind, how I would love
For it to be mine to pick apart.

Discover what you have discovered.
See the dreams you wish to uncover.
Hear about the past ones
And hope I can be your future lover.

Sitting in your heart
I feel strong as a rock.
The drum beat under my feet
Moves me; but only closer.

Sitting in your heart I find closure
Although this is only the beginning
I am so sure
That we won't have beef
This relationship will be kosher.

And even if there ever is an ending
From the time of now,
To the time of us bending and breaking
When our hearts have done too much aching.
And our bodies start to crumble from all the quaking,
The end is in sight.
But, in the morning when I'm waking.

I don't want to pack up my bags,
I don't want you to leave.
Let's rewind and replay in slow motion.
Re-find the love again.
I say with my voice shaking
"My heart is yours for the taking."

And, if you do take it.
Carve it out.
Make a home inside.
Gaze into the wonder
Outside your window.
Would you look at that view?
Now do you see what I see
In you.

It's powerful.
It's like
Lightning
Striking
Over and over again.
No, this will not be the end.

I Fall Fast

When I fall in love...I fall fast.
When I land I resemble a pancake,
And California.
It's a great way to start the day.
But, I always get burned far too easily.

My world gets flipped upside down
This always seems to happens at the wrong time.
Before I've had the chance to truly find myself,
I get pulled off life's vine
Not even halfway up the climb.
You know I'd like to say I don't mind.

The truth is, this is a vicious cycle.
I'm liable
To be lonely in the end,
Never finding that one true lifelong lover and bestfriend.

How can I, if I don't know myself?
When I fall in love
I put my feelings on the back burner,
On the top part of the shelf.
You know way up there past the lima beans
And decade old dried goods
You've saved for the next apocalypse.
The part where the sun don't shine.
That's where my emotions go, when love is on my mind.

I've let so many moments in time pass by,
By thinking about the future and past,
The ifs and the why.

If I could get them all back,
I'd have so much time to borrow.
Maybe then I could spend those extra years
Figuring out my fears,
Loving deeply, shedding a few more tears.
entwined with the joy,
Life will always have some sorrow.

You can't have the light without the dark.
After all, if you can see everything clearly,
What fun is a spark?

And before I go on let me clear just one mystery.
This isn't about any one person.
Well actually it is. It's about me.

And I think it's time I turn over a new leaf,
Ya know shed those tears and let go of this grief.

Boy doesn't that sound nice?
To actually cry for once in my life!
That's something that for a long time I've wanted.
But whenever I get to that edge
I re-find my balance on this knife
I don't know why my emotional growth has been stunted.

I don't know why.
The family I grew up in wasn't afraid of emotions,
I had loving parents,
Brothers who I loved
But sometimes didn't like very much.

So why has hiding from my truth become my crutch?
Where'd I get this, "you can't express yourself" notion?
I should be able to speak my mind,
Let fly these cursed feelings.

It would be so great if I could
Just wake up on any given day and be like hey,
I don't feel good right now and that's OKAY!
It's OKAY to cry, sometimes it will be my turn,
To let those tears fall with a shutter and a sigh.

It's OKAY to embrace it to grow and to learn.
It's not so scary, yes at first they may burn,
But no more will I lie to myself.
It continues to tie my stomach into knots
And make me feel queasy.

So yes I'm scared right now.
I know one day it will be easy
There's a chest, and the lock…
No matter how strong I've grown I can't break it.
I can only hope that it will open on its own
When it's no longer afraid of being exposed and naked.

I don't know where to go from here.
I don't know what to say.
Oh, hey,
You know what?

That's OKAY!

I think it's time this poem came to an end,
So I'm going to put down my pen
And then,
Do my best to surrender to life's joy,
But mostly to not hide away from the pain,
My friend.

First Kisses

My personal belief
Is that first kisses
Are meant to be awkward.

Because
If you can handle that,
Palms sweaty,
Knees weak,
Arms heavy,
Lips dry
and slanted at the perfectly wrong angle moment
And still want to see each other again?

Well you two just might
Have a sliver of hope for your future together.
Now I'm not saying it will happen,
Nothing is written in stone,
Well except for ancient writing
Which was of course written in stone.

But, you know what's not made of stone.

Your lips.

How's that for a Segway?

They are soft, warm, inviting.
Even when I tremble and stumble at their threshold
Even if I make a terrible first impression.

I hope I leave my mark,

Maybe you'll touch the spot that I marked,
And remember,
The awkward man,

Who said goodbye
By getting close enough to say with his lips,
What his voice could not manage.
And maybe you will touch your smile and think to yourself

"I hope he comes back to visit."

Haiku #13
Starlight in Her Smile

The moon smiled; the sea
simply could not contain it's
love any longer.

Noah Weaver

Lovely Sunday

You are more than a pretty face to me
You are a name and a place to me
You are the place where my heart last lied
You are the name that I scream when I sigh inside
You are the breath on my lips I don't want to let go
You are the moment I want to stay frozen as snow
You are the dream, I'm sad when it's time to wake up.

Of course when it's your voice,
Your touch that shakes me out of sleep,

Seeing you laying next to me
Starts my day with the strongest of heart beats.

The universe courses beneath the tips of my fingers
As they caress your neck and cheek.

Guiding my lips to you by touch,
Laughing and smiling when they meet.

We can't hold it in when we feel so much.
With you my smiles are never meek.

To you this may sound sweet or exceptionally corny,
Either way,
This is my fantasy of a lovely Sunday morning.

Badass Brunette

So I am just head over heels for this badass brunette,
The moment we met,
I knew this was *the* girl I wanted to get

To know a little bit better.
She had the three C's. Cute, competitive, and clever.
So it was never a matter of whether,

Just a matter of when,
Would our adventures begin?
As far as my heart was concerned
It was guaranteed that we would happen.

It's still hard to believe,
But, she brought my heart right out of its cage
To be worn proudly on my sleeve,
For all the world to see.

I mean look at me. What do you see?
Is this excitement? Is this glee? :D
It's all of the above.
In this sea of love, I could swim endlessly.

And, I'm afraid of water.
But, holding her hand
I can nap in the current like an otter.
It's suddenly no bother, as long as I got her

By my side. It's easy to go with the tide.
Find my stride
Even though life is a rollercoaster of a ride.
But, with her, It's smooth as an owl's easy glide.

To give you an idea of my rollercoaster.
I was supposed to be single,
Probably living in a bachelor pad
With a bed and a toaster.
I was so sure.

So set,
Just, give me two years
Before I even think about finding a girl to get,
And yet.

There she was,
The universe put this badass brunette right in my lap
And suddenly saying I needed to be single…
Well, it felt like a load of crap.
God, when it comes to romance I really am a sap.

You know what, I'm happy with that.
Us saps we have more fun in the world.
So yeah, I went from single to plural.
I can't believe it, I'm still shocked
That this badass brunette is my girl.

A Thousand Burning Suns

I said "I love you with the passion
Of a thousand burning suns".
A bit unrealistic, but you make me feel romantic,
You make me want to have some fun!

Now I'm just one human being,
So a thousand suns is beyond my abilities.
Still the sentiment is real, my love.
I will excite you with my fire
And in the same breath bring to you tranquility.

I will engulf you, as the sun will one day engulf the earth.
On the other side of our inferno is not death but rebirth.

You are worth more than diamonds, sapphires and gold.
Put together.
The word seems to fall short,
But, my dear you are a *treasure*.

And I endeavor to discover
Every side of you, my lover
What was hidden; undercover.
I will uncover under covers.
I wish for you to always feel free,
I never wish to smother.
Except with kisses,
Head to toe as we live, laughing and loving with each other.

Your smile, drives me wild,
Brings out my inner child.
I've got the feeling that we are never going out of style.

My love,
We are extremely competitive
So we'll always stay on top.
We give each other an edge
But, we'll never let each other drop.
Our love is cooler than hip hop.
It don't stop, it don't Everest, it's the precipice.
Baby, you are my mountain top.

Yet as warm and inviting to the touch as
Water in the Bahamas.
You are my vacation,
With you I find relaxation,
No stress, no dramas.

Around you I want to be my best,
Chase the passion in my chest.
For the longest time I was perplexed
About where I would go next.

Now I see it, this dream I believe it!
And, you're right by my side every stride
As a partner not a guide.
I know it's okay to fail as long as I tried.

Flower Bed

When I fall I know you'll offer a hand,
You'll pick me up again.
Help dust me off
Remind me that I've always got a friend.
I'll probably grin.

And give to you my passion like a thousand burning suns
Even when I'm feeling lost,
My darling, with you by my side I've won.

Haiku #14
Together

True love and deep trust
cannot live separately.
They would die alone.

Odds & Ends

Haiku #15
Nice to Meet You

I love Metaphors.
I've never met a forest
that I didn't like.

I'M VEGAN

Attention!
Attention everyone!
I want to let you all know that...
I'M VEGAN!

And I will happily shove that knowledge down your throats
Like the disgusting meat you consume everyday.

Because even if you're just an acquaintance,
My lifestyle must be on display
Posted front and center for the entire world to see.
Nobody shall ever offer me shark jerky again.
I was deeply offended the last time that happened.

                                    (By choosing this lifestyle
                                    I'm totally better than you.

                                    Although I'll never say it,
                            I definitely think it alllllll the time.)

Hi, remember me?
I'm vegan.

That means I don't eat meat.
No fish either,
It still has eyes, silly.

And, no dairy for me,
Milk is meant for the baby animals
You sicko.

Oh my god, are you having a birthday party today?
I'd love to come,
But I can't eat the cake *or* the ice cream.
So I'll just bring my own. And you should totally try some!
They're made from rice and after awhile they're nearly edible.
Yes both the cake *and* the ice cream. Duh.
I'm also gluten free, so they are too of course!

Because my body is a temple.
And I would not be caught dead
Putting anything as harmful as gluten in it.

Oooooo and I've cut down on all soy products too.
Soy contains a ton of estrogen.
I've read some articles
And too much estrogen in men is a bad thing.
It can cause certain problems to arise
Or um…not arise.

I don't even get why everyone doesn't just go organic.
Pesticides are killing all the cute little bugs
And slowly poisoning me. No! Thank you.

And it's a shame,
That restaurants are like
Not at all health conscious.
I *refuse* to eat out anymore.

Or eat anything that's cooked.
That takes some of the nutrients out,
And if I'm not getting it all,
Then like, why even bother?

I love sharing about my lifestyle,
Aww, and it is so refreshing that you like, love listening.
Wow It's only been like 90 seconds
But we've all gotten to know each other so well!
I love riding the subway, don't you?

Oh my god, you'll never guess!
I was going to eat a grape the other day and...
I looked it up, fruit has soooooo much sugar,
So I cut that out of my diet right away!

And grains.
Oh man, don't even get me started on grains.

I could eat veggies.
But, if I only eat veggies
I won't have a very balanced diet, will I?

I mean like,
I don't even really trust water anymore
You know,
After what happened in Flint.

Hang on I haven't ate or drank anything in days
I'm getting a bit lightheaded.
Luckily, I have just the thing for that,

It's time for dinner!

I am very excited to be able to say...
After cutting out all that nasty food stuffs,
I'm finally a pure airhead!

Takes a dinner-sized breath and nearly passes out.

Ah delicious.

Every night, as I'm falling asleep I wonder.
Will you still be alive when I wake up?

Or will you be dead,
The life drained from you.

When I wake up in the morning.
I quickly go to where you were resting,
Conserving your energy the night before,
I tap you gently.

You respond to my touch.
Oh thank goodness. There is still life in you.
You had me really worried.
You weren't responding to anything last night.

Luckily it seems that resting helped you to recharge
And gain back some of your strength.

This is a God-send, a signal from above.
You still have some time left on this earth.
The memories you hold are not yet lost to the world.
We can still look back on those moments together,
We share so many.

We both love looking back
And reminiscing about this girl.
You were a great wingman,
You facilitated so many of our meet ups.
You were with us on many of our dates.

You were a real bro.
You even saw her naked
But I knew I had nothing to be jealous of.

It's night time again.
I hook you up to your machine
Praying you don't die as I sleep.
I'm scared
I take a deep breath and close my eyes to the fear.
Wondering if you will still be here when I wake up.

Dear Phone

• ● ●

Oh no! I think the printer glitched. This poem's title was suppose to be on page 109, not 111!! Wait, WHAT! It didn't make it into the Contents section either?! Oh man this is a disaster...

Sunshine & Shade

Dreams

I dream to write,
To take these words swimming in my head at night
And create poems
That will provoke thought, provide insight.

I'm thankful for any love
You are willing to offer,
I don't exactly have a full coffer,
But with love I am rich, so it's no bother.

The starving artist is a story we've all been told,
Well my friend I would like to break that mold.
You offer me riches, I'll return them ten fold
In the form of poetic, hand woven gold.

And when I'm up on stage and thousands adore me,
I'll spin a story of glory for those who did support me.

If

Mankind

Possesses

Optimism

Something

Seemingly

IMPOSSIBLE

Becomes

Literally

Effortless

The Saga Continues

Let the saga begin.

From the outside looking in, it is great!
But, it's all skin deep man,
The smiles are thin and fake.
Weep behind closed doors,
When they open to friends,
Sweep your dirt under the rug,
Embrace them with a grin.

You begin again and the saga continues…
You've been use to abuse,
So you choose to recluse,
Hate the ahhs and oohs
It's better to lose.
Don't know what damage you'd do
If you were a cannon let loose,
So you bandage your bruise,
And drown your blues in booze.
And, you don't know why you're not happy,
You are so confused.
Then it starts once again and this saga continues.

A

Muse
Inspiring
Creation

Right Writings

Last night,
I told myself to write, write, write.
And most of it will not come out right,
Or into my heart give new insight.

But, some just might,
Those few gems,
Those diamonds in the rough,
To find them, that's why I do this stuff.

I'm going to write, write, write,
Write, and write.
Even if I never left
This life I will never get enough.

Noah Weaver

The Midnight Hour

The midnight hour is close at hand.
I feel an urge in my right hand,
An urge so right, an urge to write,
Brought to life by the wind
And the light of the moon on the land.

Mankind

They're troubled
As the present stirs up a memory of
an enemy
Who has caused so many
Of their brothers and sisters
To crumble.
The tree tops tremble
And whisper
"Mankind is coming."

Punchlines

The poetic power in this room is deafening…

Which may be why.
Many poets choose to extend their words
Through their hands to deliver their punchlines,
That they write in the crunch time.
Right before they hit the stage,
Without much time
Left to put a period on a page.
Written in red
To mimic the blood
That their heart pumped to their head.
As they prepared
What is getting ready to be read.
Putting down the final dot of lead.
Dropping the pen
To signal the end
And hitting the paper with their hand
As if to punch lines.

Waves

Water crashing
Like swords clashing,
Broken
By the armored shore.

Neptune
Sends wave after wave,
'Til the land is the sea's
Forever more.

Brightside

I was burned in the past.
Well,
Wood can't be used for fire twice.

The Quest

You fall asleep
So not a peep
Until you all awaken.

The quest goes on
Another dawn.
Though resolve is surely shaken.

The night is scary,
And you are weary,
From the troubles of the day.

You bicker and fight,
Through all the light,
And in the dark another life is snatched away.

Love?

So I am left asking
What is love?

A touch?
Or a hug?
A kiss?
Or a drug?

None of the above?

What is love?

125

Ego

Maybe it's my ego, I hope you remember my name.
I hope I impacted your lives, gave your hearts a flame.
Taught you to torch your fear, burn away your shame,
For darkness cannot grow when your light you claim.

I hope you see these things when you look in the mirror.
You see your dreams come true, be it fortune or fame,
Happiness, peace, loving the one you hold most dear,
They appeared and with them, the happiest of times came.

Look in your heart. If you chase what you hold, in there,
Your life will be a force of nature, like the sun or rain.
If people choose to frown, to bicker, snicker and sneer,
Know that they are working through their own pain.

Though the path you've chosen shall not always be clear,
Your train of thought is strong enough to maintain.
Surround yourself with the ones who always cheer,
With those who never say your passions should be tame.

Do You?

Do you laugh in the rain?
Do you go insane?
Do you prick your skin?
Numb the pain
With a needle in your vein?

Dizzy

Love will spin you so madly
It'll stop you from knowing;

Day	down,	no,
right,	from	Left
Yes	Up	night.

Love will stop you from knowing
Monday from Tuesday
And Tuesday from Saturday.

Love finds the answers for you
Outside of your scope of existence,
Until one day, she becomes your new world view.
Love makes no sense,

Yes somehow, love makes all the sense in the world.

Choices

If I could choose
I'd choose you,
Like Ash chose Pikachu.
One peek at you
I peeked my boo.
Not the time to ghost, pull a sneak on you,
Be up front, walk up and say "how do you do?"

But, in my throat there's a lump,
Stopping the words getting through.
Haven't got a clue,
What to say,
What to do.
After all
I don't want to look like a freak to you.
And,
I'll trip over my tongue trying to speak to you.

I Love You

Dear dad, dear mom,
A love letter
From your son.

You both gave me the blocks
Wooden or Lego
To build the man I've become.
You taught me it's easy to smile
If you let it be easy
Easy to make every smile genuine.

The key is to always, always, always,
Do more of what makes life fun!
You inspire me to live my life
With kindness and sincerity,
By all that you do, all that you've done.

Thank you Mom and Dad
For the world you've given me.
You've planted peace in my garden,
Those seeds still live in me.
27 years. My how time's flown.
That piece of peace in my mind,
It's amazing how it's grown.

I love you.
        Sincerely, Noah

Acknowledgements

A ridiculously huge thank you to my parents Rick and Janet Weaver for home schooling me, allowing me to learn life in my own time, in my own way. Because of your choice, my garden had acres upon acres of room to grow.

Thank you to Arianna Neal for helping edit this book and supporting my artistry. And thank you to both my mom and Arianna for the cover: my mom for the photo, Arianna for editing it. I am fortunate to know such wonderful people.

Thank you to Gemma Campanini for the beautiful foreword, it brought a tear to my eye.

Thank you to my brothers Zachary and Isaiah who have taught and continue to teach me numerous life lessons.

Thank you to all my friends for sharing with me so many awesome experiences! This book would not exist without the memories we've created together.
What's a poet without his life experiences?
What are experiences without friends?

Thank you to all the poets who I've ever encountered on the stage or otherwise! Your passion for the art is extremely contagious!

Oh, and one final thank you to every lovely being, human or otherwise who inspires poetry in me.

NOAH WEAVER is a writer, musician and game designer from the Kansas City area. He began writing and performing his poetry in 2016 as a way to heal his broken heart. The moment he stepped on stage for the very first time at Oh Snap! Poetry to read his poem, appropriately but not intentionally titled, "Moment in Time," his whole body shook with nervous excitement and the embers in his heart came roaring to life! When he got back home, Noah dove headfirst into the awesome spoken word scene of Kansas City, Missouri, writing and performing new pieces of work at a prolific rate. In 2019 he took his poetic verse into the music realm, releasing his first rap album *Never Lose Wonder* under the pseudonym N.L.W. He started using his full name in 2022 with his singles *Galaxy* and *Good Vibes*.

Noah has written over 400 pieces of poetic work in a variety of styles: free verse, limericks, haikus, rap verses and even tongue twisters. Noah started writing tongue twisters in response to his speech therapy following a serious, almost tragic car crash in 2022.

His love for words continues to grow, and going forwards Noah aims to do four words: Inspire (minds), Love (life), Create (connections) and Be (light).

"Life is poetry.
All I did was take the time to sit down and write it out."